M000297007

# Genealogy
# Lesson
# for the Laity

# Genealogy Lesson for the Laity

Cathryn Shea

Genealogy Lesson for the Laity
Copyright © 2020 Cathryn Shea
All Rights Reserved
Published by Unsolicited Press
Printed in the United States of America
First Edition Paperback.

No part of this book may be used or reproduced in any manner whatsoever
without written permission except in the case of brief quotations embodied in
critical articles or reviews.

Unsolicited Press
Portland, Oregon
www.unsolicitedpress.com
orders@unsolicitedpress.com
619-354-8005




Cover Design: Kathryn Gerhardt
Editor: Jay Kristensen Jr.
ISBN: 978-1-950730-52-0

For George, Brian, and Aimee

# Table of Contents

# Acknowledgments

My thanks to the editors and staff of the following magazines where these poems first appeared, sometimes in a different version:

*After the Pause*: "The Fabrication of Dobros"

*The Alembic*: "Thought Safe"

*Allegro Poetry Magazine*: "Green Skirts" and "Notice to Cancel Future Ski Trips"

*Amaryllis (Poetry Swindon)*: "Riven"

*(b)OINK*: "The Insect Effect and My Alma Mater"

*burntdistrict*: "Early Advice to Kindergartners," "The Postponed Grief," and "Love Bit"

*Cacti Fur*: "Epiphanies"

*Corvus Review*: "Enos is Not the Real Family Name"

*Cheat River Review*: "Practical Tips About Lightning for the People of Aleppo"

*Contemporary Haibun Online*: "An Ear Full in the Waiting Room"

*FIVE:2:ONE*: "The Wealth and Death in Mountains"

*Foliate Oak*: "A Boy's Name"

*The Ghazal Page*: "Trouble with Paper" and "Oakland"

*Ghost City Review*: "Drano Didn't Work"

*ISACOUSTIC*: "Surrounded at Pyramid Lake"

*LINES+STARS*: "Genealogy Lesson for the Laity"

*The Literary Hatchet*: "Hail Mary" and "Millville"

*Marin Poetry Center Anthology*: "R Was for Rhinoceros"

*New Orleans Review* (web feature): "Letter of Appreciation"

*Quercus Review*: "Chance of a Lifetime" (published as "Call of the Wild")

*Red Eft Review*: "Watches"

*Riggwelter*: "1.9 Cars Per Every 1.8 People"

*Rise Up Review*: "National Geographic Special"

*Schuylkill Valley Journal*: "When I Swim Alone at Night at the Motel"

*Tar River Poetry*: "Today's Advisory"

*Typehouse Literary Magazine*: "The Undercover Activity of Poplars"

*UCity Review*: "Advent People," "Anniversary," "Auden Lines," "On 'The Conjugation of the Paramecium'," and "Bone Density"

*Zetetic: A Record of Unusual Inquiry*: "Ogallala The Great Aquifer Speaks to My Grandkids"

"Early Advice to Kindergartners" was featured in *Verse Daily* and *Schuylkill Valley Journal* along with "The Postponed Grief" in *Poetry Lit Picks Vol. 1*. "Editing What the Doctors Keep Saying" was selected for *Luminous Echoes: A Poetry Anthology* by *Into the Void Magazine*. "Blowin' Cane" received an International Poetry Competition Merit Award from *Atlanta Review* in 2013.

# I.

# The Long Vigil

# Advent People

*Today, if we have no peace, it is because we have forgotten
we belong to each other...*

—Mother Teresa

We would do good
to hide candy
behind all the days
of the calendar.
To sweeten
the burden of our weeks.

Weave an emblem
of harmony in a wreath
made of evergreens.
Light infinite
many-hued candles
for the long vigil.

# Today's Advisory

The morning sprinkles powder into my eyes,
what I hope was a dream oozes out my left ear.

I tune a crystal on a wavelength stuck in gunk.
Ice on the road, the slime of life suspended.

Advisory on the ancient radio: chains required today.
I should oil that dial stuck on the weather.

The blizzard in my nightmare couldn't be real,
I should slide out of bed,

catch the tram to a wakeful state.
Where the calendar grows fat,

where I can shovel my plans into days
before they leak all over

the slush pile of intentions.
But I think there's still a bad freeze out there.

I'll just wait for my comforter
to become less viscous.

# Apology for Bad Forecasts

Our apologia tucked away in DNA
of ancestors, forecasts flirt
with weather and economies.

Belief we like to call fact
folds away for another blame
in a bejeweled, thieving month.

# Family Tree

A roiled reach of shoal beyond the Gate,
the surge, descent,
and resurrection of orphaned timber.

The tide reverses, fosters erosion
of the cliffs. Shifts the silt
of the ocean floor and beach.

My family tree floats out there
part of so much flotsam,
branches sheared off in the waves.

I was born twenty miles from this
grave of shipwrecks, where gulls eye
fertile tide pools from the rocks.

The acorn that grows from earth to heaven
is a story told a different way for each new life.
Family tree in shadow and fog.

What it shows is always the same. Family
photos in boxes: *Stand to one side. No, come closer.*
The scenes in albums are serene.

Old tree, made up of missing answers,
I shall never put you together in one piece.
Your testaments lost in fire and flood, war and want.

# Early Advice for Kindergartners

Learn from the praying mantis,
be reincarnated as a blue-belly lizard.
Flit into an underworld where shadows
sort themselves and sprout.

Be suspect if you're blindfolded a lot.
You can't understand what I'm saying yet.
You might be living in a bad neighborhood
or in a euphemism for war.

# Editing What the Doctors Keep Saying

Your diagnosis, with its errors and typos, the variations of your genes,
cast like a molten Linotype slug.

The gene sequence spelled with its *etaoin shrdlu*[1] in the vocabulary of GATC:
guanine (G), adenine (A), thymine (T), cytosine (C)

Will we both be gone when the mutations are known?
Grief engraves that health thief, punctuates my thoughts with gaps of sadness,
more like punctures the beliefs we cleave to,

the trials, the cures, medical glossaries swirling over my head,
language I don't understand, no relief in the cryptic words of the prognosis.

"Stay in the present," the key to panic
avoidance. *Escarole-ay* when I can't remember
the author's name. I mean Eckhart Tolle. Yes,
follow his advice and stay in the day, the now.
Oh, read to get drowsy, to distract from worry
before bedtime. Read until
sleep takes over.

For now, we are alive with the printed page,
lost in worlds of words.

---

[1] Etaoin shrdlu (pronounced *eh-tay-oh-in shird-loo*) is a nonsense phrase that sometimes appeared in print in the days of "hot type" publishing because of a custom of type-casting machine operators to run their fingers down the left-side vertical rows of keys of the Linotype keyboard when they knew they made an error or typo.

# An Ear Full in the Waiting Room

The doctor is absent, not a hint of her presence as I sit fifty minutes going on how many more, unknown. The parking meter holds my many coins, grudgingly deposited to yield two hours. Surely, this appointment will not require more time than I purchased on the street patrolled by the career meter person. *Cerumen*, from Latin for wax. I inherited the trait of hard ear wax from my grandfather on my mother's side, according to my cousin. Wax builds up in my left ear canal as I wait. I feel its insidious permeation and expansion, its plan to render me trapped by the sensation of my head squeezed against a sound-proof window. Maybe the doctor has prejudged this request for ear washing a frivolous nuisance. Perhaps the appointment before me was an embolism[2]. I should be grateful I have ears at all.

       sunlight's candle
       hot on sidewalk
       loud blue sky

---

[2] Embolism: (ĕm′bə-lĭz′əm)
    i. (Medical) obstruction of an artery, typically by a clot of blood or an air bubble.
    ii. (Timekeeping) an intercalation of a day or days in the calendar to correct error.
    iii. An intercalated prayer for deliverance from evil coming after the Lord's Prayer.

# Remnants of Star Death

Common element of betrothals and marriage
until death does its part, infernal diamonds
spewed from Earth's innards,
borne in magma through kimberlite pipes,
dispersed in disastrous diasporas
over deltas and plains.

True or False:
Carbon atoms come from dead stars.
(Atoms in a diamond or a tree or me?)
Older than our solar system.

There's our great-aunt's legendary
five-carat, cushion-cut rock
set in Art Deco platinum, said to be
from her heavenly spouse.
Removed from her ossified finger,
the jewel eludes heirs.

So much carbon among us, a fine line
between graphite in pencils
and big ice at pawn shops.
How many believe
they are forever?

# Great-Great-Grandmother's Green Skirts

*after tunes on* Open Hearth *by*
*Mary and Andrew MacNamara*

The green-gowned girl bound for California,
teal feathers sewn to her collar,
irises iridescent as prisms.
A bag of spuds peeled and left behind.
*I'm leaving the harvest, leaving home*
*before the morning star sets*, she murmurs
for the boy in the woods who's fast asleep
in his bed, blood and lymph not bestirred
except when dreams take him to her.
Glad she's not in bad humor,
her mood not melancholy, she whispers
*Holy Mother*, sighs the sign of the cross.
Vapors falter over the bog like steam
from the kettle she boiled earlier.

# Riven

She was born with a bad gene.
Penury they call it. Lack.
Passed through the blood,
indigence hidden in her DNA.
The mutation she couldn't escape.

She belonged to one of those
defective family trees, a loser
in a fitter family contest.
She wasn't a blue-ribbon baby
like a prize calf or grand pumpkin.
More like a bumpkin
that would devolve the species.

This knack for being poor
snuck through the gauntlet of heredity.
The state tried hard to keep her mother
from breeding. Before
they tied her tubes.

So here she is today, torn
from an expectant history.
She wears ripped jeans,
has no means.
Her brain may not be
bad. She learns
a new word

every day. Every day
a new word,
like *riven.*

# Chance of a Lifetime

*San Francisco, at the present time, is like the crater of a volcano,*
*around which are camped tens of thousands of refugees.*

–Jack London

The boom is at its apex and I take N Judah
the last leg of my commute
along Embarcadero to the foot of 3<sup>rd</sup>
where Pac Bell Park screeches its coliseum shape
into existence, honeycombed with scaffolding,
hard hats swarming jack-hammered sidewalks.

Plywood tunnels guide me past the burnt-pork smell
of the drive-through donut place, past granite façades
to my job where the dotcom startup bristles
with important confusion: wine going online,
Napa Valley delivered to Iowa tax-free.

On my lunch break, down the street I find
a marble plaque embedded like a lonely headstone
in the defunct Wells Fargo branch,
marking Jack London's birthplace.

His mother's story long forgotten. How she tried
suicide, abandoned by her lover, pregnant
and penniless. The small revolver's bullet
deflected, she accepted (grudgingly)
Nancy Slocum's generosity and shelter,

gave birth right at this spot, in peace
out of wedlock. I don't think she'd care
that the Bay is silted in under the construction zone,
a creek named after excrement flows

where the beach was.
I care that Jack London was born here,
was almost not born anywhere.


The rising baseball stadium disavows scandal
before a Giant even spits on the new sod,
disowns its birth name like a runaway.
Its being will shift with the inevitable trembling
under the city's relentless
renewal.

# Epiphanies

I had an epiphany today:
Stay calm
and don't ask
for answers.

I wanted a magical telephone
to dial me up and announce,
"This is college calling. We've
decided your major."

Then I would fall asleep
and in the morning I'd know
with certainty what career
I'd be hired for.

A bird would descend from
heaven and chirp in my ear
to confirm my choice of mate.
"Yes, this person is to be
a good spouse."

Somehow, I would know to have
a child at age 25. Ring, ring.
The doorbell sounding. It's
a package!

Someone said to imagine
a question about any problem
at bedtime and sleep on it.
The best solution
would reveal itself
in the morning.

I wanted epiphanies
for hard decisions:...
Move? Buy the house? Rent?
Quit this job? Have another
child? Leave my husband?
Stay with my husband?

Try harder to fall asleep
in the middle of all this...?

# Enos is Not the Real Family Name

i

I'm walking in Provincetown
and I notice the name Enos on mailboxes,
then I see "Portuguese bread here"
and when I stop for lobster bisque
I see on the menu "Portuguese baked clams."
Because, my friend tells me, Azores Portuguese
settled here, and I think of my maternal grandfather,
Anthony Victor Enos, explaining when I was young
his parents came from peculiar sounding
islands, Pico and Faial.

I try to release myself from the distraction
of the picture window looking out on the charming harbor
where Enos seems to be everywhere
so I can remember what I've been told as a child.

ii

For what I can't remember, I devise a past of how my grandfather and his sisters
drove to California in a black Model T, each packing one suitcase to hold
everything dear. I can only project grainy images of them laughing and worrying
their way across the Great Plains and Rockies. Their parents, my great-
grandparents, came through Ellis Island and settled in Providence, Rhode Island,
a place I've still never been in my life because the priority of visiting my
grandfather's birthplace got buried in the grind of marriage, motherhood, and
job. And now I'm visiting the east coast for the first time and in my skewed sense
of geography, I thought Providence was right next door to my friend's town with
its art galleries and knickknacks on Commercial Street.

iii

My grandfather blamed the government
for indifference to immigrants,
their family origins and traditions.
The customs officers assigned Enos
to multitudes of Azores Portuguese.

He kept saying he loved his father's true surname.
Oliveira for olive tree, he would have
Americanized it to Oliver. "Enough Enos,"
he swore, his olive skin turning red
with this resentment he took to his grave.

iv

If I could talk to my grandfather now, I would tell him what I found out. Myriad
Azorean boys were christened the same middle name after patron saint Ignatius.
Enos is from Inácio, which Azores Portuguese pronounced *ee-NAHs*.

v

My grandfather's father Antonio Ignacio Oliveira
accepted the new family name for the new country
he was entering, the new life in Providence.
I must steal from other stories, other Enos histories
and merge the made-up with the supposed facts,
which I can never know.

"Great-Grandfather was a whaler,
Great-Grandmother was a tailor"
immortalized in fragments of family tales,
daily details of strife vague,
harpoons and thimbles lost.

# Genealogy Lesson for the Laity

The genome of my aunt is in the family.
Straitlaced, she drank gin
from under the sink, worked hard,
flew in the sky and was forlorn.
Did you know her?

She lived in all our neighborhoods.
We loved to solve her crosswords
and steal rhubarb tarts
and sneak a peek at her rubber girdle.

It was a hard lesson for an eighteen-year-old.
I could be sassy and she'd slap the song out of my lungs.
Her old bromides aside, gloom could tread and tread
our tangles and tug at her hem.

I buried my key to her house
in the skirts of the weeping willow.
Spring nailed its velvet wrist
to my outstretched arm.

# II.

# Bones of Steel

# Bone Density

*I threw the bone toward that incessant claiming...*

—Claudia Emerson, "Bone"

We must release our bracelets,
slide rings off, unclasp watches,
remove keys from pockets,

or the bone density test
will convince itself
we're made of steel.

# Change of Life

*for T*

The one doctor you trust with your gut
examines you like you're a man,

none of that female equipment
to complicate his view.

This leads to a battery of tests,
all of which confirm there is nothing wrong

with your gastrointestinal pipes.
Your bloating is just gas

and you should give up
gluten, eat kale, and go Paleo.

You're driving home months later
listening to a talk about ovaries on public radio.

You feel queasy, a bit nauseated
at what you've just heard.

You make an appointment
with your gynecologist.

This leads to a battery of tests,
all of which confirm there is something wrong

with your reproductive organs.
Your bloating is a mass

and you should give up
your vacation plans.

So, you enter the hospital and wake up
the next day without female equipment.

Your health plan has physicians competing.
One fears you'll die too soon,

another claims you're a survivor.
They agree you need treatment and drugs,

can't tell you for how long, can't tell you
how your life will change.

# My Grandmother's Bosom

She bound her chest
with an Ace bandage
because she couldn't afford
a proper side-lacer brassiere
and her breasts were too ample
for the drop-waist flapper shift she was after,
the androgynous, schoolboy flatness
all the rage.

The tight binding ruined her
muscles she said when I asked
why her breasts sagged on her middle.
I was little and used to bothering her
with inappropriate questions. She looked
different in her nightie and I worried
about her body's droop,
different from what I was used to
in her aproned house dress.

\* \* \*

When I was about to have my first child,
I wanted to know
if she breastfed my mother.
*No*, she said. Formula was ultramodern,
forward, freeing up time
that might otherwise have been spent
nursing out of sight
hidden from prying eyes, judgments
expressed in reproof:
*Is baby getting enough?*

She and my mother were captivated
by what I told them about La Leche League
helping parents, families, whole communities
to breastfeed, chest feed, human milk feed
their babies.

Breastfeeding was radical, paradoxically
avant-garde to them. They wanted me to
succeed but they couldn't resist worrying,
blurting out the question that nagged them:
*Is baby getting enough?*

\* \* \*

Determined for her baby to thrive
on her breastmilk, my daughter
became anxious when he didn't latch,
his little mouth scrunching and sucking air.
Heating the hated formula, just in case,
how we scurried about, frantic
in between coaxing him onto nipple,
weighing, checking diapers,
anxious about his tongue's frenulum.
Plagued by worry:
*Is baby getting enough?*

I bought her Guinness stout because
that's what boosted my milk supply.
Baby still struggled at her breast.
*Fenugreek seed has been used to increase
milk production since biblical times,*
said the lactation consultant.
Three capsules three times a day.
Add tincture of blessed thistle,
twenty drops three times a day.
Then domperidone, three tablets

three times a day. My daughter sated
on herbal remedies while I sipped
bubbly wine.

We drove all over creation
gathering prescribed ingredients.
My daughter devoted her day
and night to the regimen
while milk leaked and squirted,
her breasts overflowing.
My grandson gulping
and spitting up.
*Is baby getting enough?*

# The Hospital Cafeteria Like an Apse

The self-serve tabernacle glows
with its hot dogs, tofu burgers,
and chicken nuggets
looking like they've incubated
for a week swaddled in foil.

A little altar set up with more self-serve:
chimichangas, tortilla bricks
next to squiggly pasta in cream of mushroom
with green peas scattered on top.

Another repast comes and goes.
A lonesome prayer
over this food, this day.

The hospital cafeteria with its inexplicable food,
crumbs on tables, understaffed help
renders sanctuary from
the worry and obsessive cleanliness
of my friend's sterile surroundings

where she has lost her appetite.
Nutrients drip into a port
in her chest. She naps
then wakes to fret, then naps again.
The wait steeps in my coffee cup.

This is the refuge from the fact of my friend
in her private room. Suffering from Neutropenia,
low white blood cell count, from treatments
that might yet
burst into a joyous cure.

# Ominous Pendant

*for my sister Nancy*

Mid-morning, Interstate 80
an ice pick in her right temple,

the traffic lanes smolder
red like runway edge lights.

She's a comely brunette,
her shade right for every occasion.

No roots visible
on that day. That f*****g day

on her way to the doctor.
She swears when she is late.

Three days before, she complained
to her hairdresser of a migraine.

Her head enshrined in pain.
This private aura, our sun eclipsed.

Her car coming to rest in a celestial field.
The circle of Willis. We never knew

it existed. A connection severed.
A bellied balloon ruptured.

We remain early in our grief.
She is late.

Is it consoling to learn
a defect is congenital?

# Watches

It's no longer acceptable to wear a wristwatch,
you must tell time by the shadows
cast on buildings and trees.

You are not allowed to look at your phone,
that would be rude.

Prove that you can navigate the world
without props and aids.

Use your head.

Imagination is a peculiar clay,
infinity captured
in the dark matter we don't understand.

The poet dies in her sleep.
And I'm jealous
because that is a good way to go
and I fear I might linger.

My grandfather told me
his ticker was winding down.
He felt it. I planned to visit soon.
Within the clock's twenty-four hour sweep
his heart stopped.

# The Postponed Grief

*after Celest Ng,* "Everything I Never Told You"

I wanted to hold back the chaos of tears,
plug the mother-shaped hole in my universe.

The laundry basket swollen
in the back seat of her car.

Hope penciled in the margins
of her cookbook.

The rug dented with the ghost
of her couch.

# Dear Larson

Do you remember your cartoon with the two bucks
in the forest? Of course, you do.

One has a target with a bullseye on its chest.
"Bummer of a birthmark, Hal," the other buck says.

I gave my father this coffee cup for Xmas
a long time ago. He laughed and laughed.

His fishing and hunting buddy Adrian roared too
on his visits back then, aluminum boat

with Evinrude outboard strapped to the top
of his F-150's camper shell.

Ade brought grocery bags full of cheese puffs,
jerky, peanuts, and pop, not to mention

fifths of Beam and plenty of ice.
My dad supplied the cribbage board, decks of cards,

and marbled beef to throw on the coals
if weather permitted. If not, on the iron skillet.

I'm recalling when I bought that gift at Target
reading every comic on every mug

for what seemed like an eternity. Howling
until a torrent of tears ran my mascara.

I swear a kid in red vest came up and said,
"Bummer, lady. Did you lose something?"

# The Short Straw

"You drew the short straw," we loved to say
not thinking it was cruel, laughing hard
especially at the person holding
the losing wisp of stalk.

I go for a mammogram and wonder
will I draw the short straw? Who would I tell?
Would I continue to live the same
and laugh at being a loser?

When my best friend drew the straw
of ovarian cancer she blamed herself
for taking hormone replacements,
blamed her mother's genes.

She went for genetic counseling, something
I had already done. We both tested negative
for known mutations. She kidded,
"I drew the short straw." We tried to laugh.

We argued nothing she had done was to blame,
the cells in her were following a random path
to ultimate anarchy. I thought of reckless behavior
when we were younger

that could have ended a life:
hitchhiking at night alone, smoking
drug-laced pipes, driving cars with bald tires
packed with screaming kids—

So many ways the short straw had been on the brink.
The day before she died, she squeezed my hand,
whispered in the faintest voice, *somebody* inaudible
"…fucked up."

# Notice to Cancel Future Ski Trips

I got a text from my mother's cruciate ligament,
anterior to be precise. It's cross-shaped.
Reminds me of The Crucifix
but that's just parochial guilt tormenting me.

As I was saying, anterior cruciate ligament
of my mother's right leg, Cruciate for short,
texted me early when I was limping from bed
to warn that I should not plan

any skiing this winter on steep slopes
in below-freezing Sierra cement,
perhaps not ski at all for the remainder of
you-know-what.

Cruciate did not want to hurt
my feelings, probably walked
on eggshells to avoid upsetting me,
knowing well enough to fear

I might still expect to schuss like I did
twenty-plus years ago over moguls
in slush and ice at breakneck speed
straight down the fall line

on outdated equipment. *Give it up*,
Cruciate says. *The next time you fall
I tear for good. You got
your mother's knees.*

# Vivarium Life

Through the glass sliding door
in my fishbowl condo
for all to see

me in my flannel nightie
chewing burnt bagels,
sheepskin slippers pacing the rug,
clips holding back my hair,
head down, nose pointing
to the floor as if I seek
Earth's molten core.

I'm not in total misery.
I'm weary of my aquarium head:
memories of my mom
swimming endless laps,
I miss her.

I miss every parent, grandparent, sister,
aunt and uncle, cousin, friend, every
cat, dog, fish, and bird that's gone before.
I miss my mother.

She climbs. Pulls herself up the ladder,
swan dives into an Olympic-size pool,
her feet pointing to pines
reflected at the deep end
where I long to caress her face.

# Bathing My Friend

*for T*

Coral-painted toenails bright,
her feet silvery black as mercury.
When the hospice nurse lifted
the thin flannel exposing her back
I saw how the body
peeled away from her spirit,
her right sole arched.
How her heels sprouted wings.

# Latin for Truth

Like a pin prick, a furtive pinch.
*Veritas*, the word from a dead language

from a pontificated past
that still affects this life.

Sharp as my parents' reprimand
piercing my scruples like a hook.

I ignore the gawking crowd,
just a predicament of urban propinquity.

Can't stop kissing the wrong people
no matter how ruinous.

# III.

# Conjugation

# On "The Conjugation of the Paramecium"

*This has nothing*
*to do with*
*propagating,*

Muriel Rukeyser said in her poem.

Today I am observing western pond turtles,
many orders beyond the paramecium.
Desire for renewal hides beneath a carapace.
Deep inside the female
inseminated cells divide.

# The Undercover Activity of Poplars

I caught them this dawn
blinking their leaves in code.

The way they touched. I knew
they were exchanging intimacies.

Their fluttering entranced me,
turned pages in my brain and I entered

this pulp romance of a past lover
tumbling in oat grass. Chambray shirt

unbuttoned, me spread like a picnic,
back sticky with sap.

Then my poplars let go and tipped their crowns
in a hasty farewell when you woke up.

And I said hello to the mounting sun,
our day just swelling.

# At the Camp in French Guiana

My first husband is long gone
from his archaeological digs
when he was a professor after
our separation and divorce,
gone from where did they say
he collapsed? At the end of a day
bushwhacking and trudging
through rainforest. It was sudden,
when he heard the final dinner bell
as he entered a clearing to a tent
in French Guiana, a place of which
I'm ignorant, years having passed
since I last saw him. Students loved
him, I'm told, and his second wife.

My now-husband hates, hates
to hear any mention of he who came
before. We can't speak of that man.
Too much. Enough, enough.
But sometimes I have a strong desire
to tell how when Steve and I were
mere teens we parked
on a red dirt road amid manzanita,
how he had a nagging hunch
his heart would give up, how
I dreaded talk about what
he thought would be
the abrupt end.

We never had children together.
And he and his second wife
never had children.

# The Falls of Idaho Falls

After my backpacking in the Panhandle of Idaho, a long winding drive with a potential mate deposited me in that iron-griddle part of Idaho, rusty with empty train-tracks, hollowed out cars, washing machines wrecked in fields. I felt cheated when I saw the namesake falls shaped like a big old horseshoe. Seemed like they were as high as the curb in the dead downtown. No place open for a bite. *Are you Indian?* a guy at the rental office asked the next day while secretaries gawked. *I don't mean American Indian*, he said. *You know...from India?* A Californian might as well be. Sitting cross-legged on my braid. That must've completed the image of me as some Hindu princess. The places I wished we could rent were landmark log cabins with sunken yards, built by pioneers. Not available. Not to an exotic like me, anyway, about to shack up with the town's new music teacher. We wore dime store bands on our ring fingers, entwined arms, gazed at each other. Finally, a landlord bought the idea we were newlyweds. We got the basement in a cinder block duplex, our potential as husband and wife failing month-to-month like the rent while we argued and fussed in the dreary dark of sub-zero winter. The falls might eventually arouse wonderment. In a million years they might become a new Niagara.

# Love Bit

That night in the cave of Lovejoy basalt.
In no shape for this tryst, we hauled a quilt
up the sheer trail, skidding on scree.
He commanded, keg-drunk, *We have to
do this*. If I drove home instead, I didn't love him.

Damp moss for a mattress, midges nipped
at our thighs. The love act spent
swatting and rubbing, condensation
dripped on us. We separated for good
the next year. Bugs flew off with our blood.

# High School Refugee

Your whisper, syncopated words, curious
inflections wavering. Your intention eluded me,
the telephone chirped like a parakeet. Then
your note arrived hard to decipher,
my attempt to interpret a weak stab.

We disliked the creaky bus that delivered us
to our daily bout with Chaucer, slumped
at reminders about posture.
"Stupid" my frontispiece to the principal,
"Question authority" we would insist later.

The school's minute hand shaped like a thunderbolt
diligently crept on its journey unattended.
I would shadow you along sidewalks
until you agreed to involve your studies with mine,
to become entangled in eglantine, the sweetbrier
of our making.

# Range of Love for an Ex

Why did we break up?
Let's not cry over why.
Words fence in the range
where I would stray
while I ruminate
in my random way.
When I used to graze
in the palm of your hand,
you were careful to be tender
and later I would stand
while you arranged
a comfortable spot on the divan.
Together we smiled
on our cat, the ambassador
from Siam, too fat,
a sly negotiator,
playful diplomat.
There were the times
when the cat was Equator,
you as North surveyed
the refrigerator
while I, the tepid South,
played caterer.
How well our household went!
You mowed the lawn,
I stirred the soup
and stifled a yawn.
The cat doesn't even know
I'm gone.

# Frozen Chops

I guess we are not going to dinner after all,
to that French restaurant you mentioned this morning
when I said I would put the lamb chops out
to thaw for tonight

and you told me not to because it might be fun
to eat over there and then go
hear our friends the Gas Men play.
I'll make reservations, you said.

I so anticipated
we were going to eat at the French place
next to the pub, and we'd laugh
and uncharacteristically become captivated
by escargot, escarole, and existentialism.

Now, dinnertime has come.
You mill around our garage with your profusion
of wrenches when we might instead be dining
at a candlelit table,
had you meant what you said.

And I stare at the deep freeze,
interactions of baffling chemistry
causing me to wonder
what makes it work.
The chops in their butcher paper
slumber in our kitchen tundra.

# Drano Didn't Work

Roy's Sewer Service is here
and from the roof of this
two-story we call home
but don't own, Roy himself
(no, it couldn't be Roy
because the guy up there
just grunts Yep and Nope,
he's sweaty in worn pants,
he isn't listening to a word I'm saying,
and wouldn't Roy himself at least act
as if he cared about my opinion?)...
Let's say, a man who I wish were
Roy himself
is shoving a clean-out rooter
down the maw of this house,
which has accumulated
many years of cloggage
(is that a word like
"baggage" is a word?)
and the walls
resound and groan
and all I can think is
this place
is going to have
one very
sore
throat.

# Anniversary

*after Robert Pinsky, "Antique"*

I tripped on the path
chasing you, I fell
at the glimmer
of not catching you,
we merged
for decades in rooms
outside towns
with snarled roads
and we chafed against
our tangled lives.

# Blue Plate Special

What starts out blue and ends up red like a Valentine? Set before me tonight at the famous place on Beale Street, chicken-fried steak and mashed potatoes poking from country gravy like little vacation spots. My nose decides to act up like it hasn't done since eighth grade. The blood won't clot, even with pinching. My nurse sister tries to help, coaxing me to drop my head. The couple from Ohio moves to a faraway table. W.C. Handy plays, flies hit the windows. The waitress rushes over with ice and white towels that are going to stain. "Sorry," she says. "We don't have any colored ones." Aunt and sister dote. My husband holds my purse, looks into my damp eyes and says, "I love you even though you're the worst tourist."

    mockingbird scolds
    fat tomato
    skin flushes

# For Husband at 3:00 a.m.

I disparage his extra drink, smoking
herb, snoring—conked out on some off-label
antihistamine that offers deep sleep
for him and none for me, nor any human
on our block. I stifle my scolding. Life
without him would be bad, I don't wish him
dead. I'd rather not be his widow.
The prominent Adam's apple of youth
when we fell in love, now soft under
adipose layers. I admire his face
and chins. The rounded shoulders and belly,
his climbing the ladder to change a bulb.
Glad for these untold years spent as a pair
I pull the covers up and smooth his hair.

# A Boy's Name

You could make your son a criminal
just by baptizing him the wrong name
seemed like the gospel truth

when I heard gossip for a long time about Caryl Chessman
on death row, my mom and her friends saying
all forms of that man's name are bad.

When my son was born, I waited three days before calling him
the name I'd looked up, having checked history and roots
and Biblical references: Brian, for strong.

"That's perfect," a nurse said, growing impatient
but doing a good job hiding her eagerness
to get on with it, raising

her brow ever so slightly while overheard saying,
"As if a name could make or break a child's
destiny."

"Why'd you name him that for?"
(My mother-in-law when we tell her.)
"That's Irish. He'll grow up to be a bum."

# When I Swim Alone at Night at the Motel

The pool becomes my own Pacific.
I become Ariel in a glistening mermaid tail.
Lips full crimson, I wear a bra made of shells,
makeup stays put not bothered by water,
my profuse auburn hair sleek in the waves.
When I swim at night alone, I can hold my breath
for five minutes, fizzy bubbles follow me
as I dart around blowup coral reefs.
I remember to exhale.

My tail slides off and I turn into a starfish
coifed in brunette curls, with thick eyelashes
on a rouged face. Then I morph into a halibut,
my slick body flattened against the ocean floor,
eyeshadowed mascaraed eyes staring up.
The tide tries to pull me out to the other end
of the miracle mile where Ken's Carpets
and Urban Smoothies line up, cars zoom past
as I cling to the rocky bottom until
the current calms down.

Back home in the above-ground pool,
I dog paddle, wear goggles and floaties.
Bob my head up and down, gasp for air,
get water up my nose. My flippers splash
too much and I make little kids scream.
The pool needs cleaning.
And no matter how hard I kick,
I stay in the same place.

## Vesta Speaks

My fireplace acts up, spills smoke
into the living room instead of up the flue—
Out pops a goddess, head wrapped in Hermès
babushka. "Do I know you?"
(Her posture seems familiar.)

"Yes and no. There were never true statues of me,
and no portraits. I wouldn't sit still.
What's that lewd noise?" The teapot vents
on the stove, whistles
only for us to hear.

"I wouldn't exist if the plebs didn't exalt me.
I could have been quiet—unheard and unknown,
nothing revealed to forget.

Today I do everything myself,
no wholesome girls to help me—
Patrician families scarcely procreate,
the urban rich raise spoilt brats,
and the suburbanites mimic them.

Now, at what age do girls become unchaste?
They remind me of rouged-up Roman women
in goat hair wigs, scary lamp-black eyebrows,
faces daubed with lead paste.
Lethal cosmetics hastened their dementia!"

So, this is Vesta of the Vestal Virgins. Homeless,
living in my chimney. She weeps.

"I had a cloistered life some millennia ago
confined to the foyer, sometimes a closet.
(Blessedly, never claustrophobic.)
My helpers and I endured the order
daughters must tend the family hearth 24/7.
Boys would piss on the fire."

Broom for a scepter, I curse the dying flame—
shoo her sooty divine butt back up the stack,
wave my vacuum wand.

# The Insect Effect and My Alma Mater

I'm not saying where
but two undergrads died
of alcohol poisoning,
a fraternity went into
the porno business,
and riots broke out
at Fifth and Ivy.

A midge drowned in my eye,
its body flown into me.
A gelatinous wreck
on a saline sea.

Waves of schnapps slosh
in my mother soul
and I cry mid-sentence.
A smutty thrust of genitals
intrudes on my grocery list
and I forget to buy milk.
I see cops with paintball guns.
My arms sting, my ears ring.

There, there. A calm
grabs me by the sleeve.
I kneel down for lunch with the bugs
where the sky has been sewing
café curtains trimmed
with rickrack. A fluffy
caterpillar drops into my salad,
ravenous for the lettuce.

# IV.

# Baffling Crime

# Auden Lines

*The situation of our time*
*Surrounds us like a baffling crime*

                      —W.H. Auden, "New Year Letter," 1940

...the homes I warm to /though seldom wealthy, always convey a feeling /of bills being promptly settled /with checks that don't bounce.

For us whose dreams are odorless, what is real seems a bit smelly.

Even our most myopic have good enough vision for courtship.

Here's my brother-in-law's ex-wife "L":

When he is well
she gives him hell,
she throws a brick
when he is sick.

# Letter of Appreciation

I am no small giver to small charities.
In spite of "A mind is a terrible thing to waste"
on this ornate letter

with its flowery "thank you" for something
someone has imagined I've done or am about to do,
I am sending no money today.

Not even the reply I'm thinking: "Ink, paper, and postage
are terrible things to waste."
And on behalf of every bright child, I am crumpling up

and discarding this misplaced praise with its machined
deckle edge and cliché in gold laser-printed lettering,
but I'll keep the address labels that came with it.

My own children dropped out of college.
One, after he broke an ulna and had mono
and questioned the reason for living,

the other after she told me on the phone
she hated her roommate, her classes, and teachers.
Essentially, hated the whole world.

I went to college and worried I wasted my mind
but got a degree anyway. I must have failed
to teach my children

not to be afraid to waste their minds.
Or maybe they saved their minds
for some other time.

# The Community Effort

Not too unlike the oak and eucalyptus
that sprout in your yard
(maybe not a great simile) you show up
gratis, uninvited perhaps or gently coerced,
or strong-armed by a charismatic person
or charming acquaintance, or maybe
it's in your DNA to help,

get the work done.
Taking money at the door, hauling in cakes and cookies,
fizzy water and wine, you become a waddling cornucopia
spreading your bounty on the folding tables
with paper plates and plastic forks
plentiful, to be reimbursed
at some point in the future, after you've floated
the check for the goods for the gala or humble event
which everyone hopes will be well-attended by patrons
or members, or drop-ins, because that is what it takes to keep
the funds flowing somehow for the nonprofit
with its tax exempt status and

mission statement. You got to have a mission
that enriches the community.
Otherwise, why
would this body of people and to-do lists
even exist? Well, no need to answer
just yet because we are all very busy on the budget and
our committee reports are due at our next board meeting.

So, hang in there, know that people will help you,
you are not alone, there is plenty of support
and expertise to back you up as you struggle
with calendars and resources

(which are people, you know). People you know.
There's no need break down and fall apart,
because you're driven
to help. Because
you're a volunteer.

# Surrounded at Pyramid Lake

Ghost horse galloping madly in the greasewood,
Eugene Angel's soul escapes
a petrified pillar of salt,
ascends the eroded cliffs above the Truckee.
Painted Paiute kicked his bones off their sacred tufa.

Sun poisoned miners
drunk on whiskey and lack of sleep
raped two Paiute girls
and this act ignited the Battle of Pyramid Lake.

Following Comstock miner hordes
by a hundred years,
here come tech people on their way to Burning Man,
bare except for boots crushing
calcifications around the sulfurous hot springs.

Two decades before, accused of public nudity
breasts smeared with clay,
hair snagged in the zipper of my cutoffs,
I'm hauled in for indecent exposure.

(Except no one saw me, save my ex).
The charges were dropped in Reno
by a one-armed judge.
The spook gelding haunted my dreams
with sympathetic pain.

# Trouble with Paper

I didn't feel smart. Always: Her messy desk, rat's nest of paper.
I could keep socks paired, spice sorted. Not paper—

Stand in front of class, repeat: My desk is messy. Feel the heat
from brain and heart blister your face. I'm messy with paper—

He couldn't manage. You're smart, I told my son. He felt stupid.
What's all this? Stuffed in his closet and under his bed, paper—

You're smart, I told my daughter. Smart. She felt dumb
as her bent-elbow Barbies, clueless dolls swimming in paper—

Receipts and bills crumpled in shoe boxes. I can't do our taxes!
What's to become of us? My love, please wait to recycle the paper.

# 1.9 Cars Per Every 1.8 People

The news triumphantly blares:
Cars have finally overtaken Population.

The vehicles I've owned outright
or shared jointly with boyfriends and husbands
constitute a politically incorrect, unpatriotic assemblage.

There was the Volkswagen (common folk buggy) from post-
post-war that rolled, didn't maim, let me climb out
through its crunched sunroof. Somehow, I'm still here.

There were the Saabs 99 and Turbo from Sweden,
one free-wheeling precursor of automatic, the other
fuel-injected-ice-grabbing. The 99, my bridal carriage
to second marriage. Both sickened at high altitudes
where we happened to live.

Peugeots (2) from France with their stinky fuel
and backward engines. Poor kids strapped in, hauled
frantically in search of diesel.

Chief Cherokee (one native American that snuck in,
this model's name a slur). After a few years of bad mileage
we paid a hit man to send Chief to the great bone yard.

The Japanese contingent: Mitsubishi, Toyota, Subaru
which could fast 20,000 miles between oil changes,
which were pronounced Totaled by insurance.
Scoffing at this prognosis, one was salvaged.

BMW, post-Berlin wall, which my husband gave me
after he had his way with it. Arrested me on Hwy 17
at the canyon's edge when I ricocheted
off the divider (so glad it was there).

Our fractured freeways.
The empty carpool lane expects me to try
not to drive alone.

# Accidental Seconds

The clothesline festooned with feeders.
Mesh cylinder, birdseed ball,
white sock full of Niger seed.

The variety of cracked this and that.
Corncobs tied to the lemon tree
spilling kernels on the ground.

My yard speckled many colors.
The diversity of birds mingling
against the background of mulch.

Seeds germinate, open tender cotyledons.
A flock of mourning doves peck,
startle, and settle again.

Crows and scrub jays vie for peanuts,
bury their prizes under twigs
and loot each other's stash.

A covey of quail calls
at dawn and late afternoon.
Their young fledge on concrete steps.

Band-tailed pigeons show up, relatives
of the extinct passenger pigeon.
Wary, anxious to fill their gullets.

Cooper's hawk swoops
onto spotted towhee. Moments
before it had been dancing in dirt.

In my dream garden
the towhee survives, ascends
to a posthumous life.

# Blue Gum

Miracle trees, eucalyptus. Seedlings pinched from primeval
forests, packed in mean ships bound for U.S. ports.
Welcomed with outstretched palms. Strike it rich!
Questionable hardwood with hemp-like bark,
lanceolate leaves oozing medicinal oil.

The cult of *Eucalyptus globulus* preached salvation
through this genus: cheap fuel, cleansed air, healing salve
from the sap. Eucalyptol, their sacred unguent,
smelling up the whole place.

On the California coast these alien trees steadily propagated.
Every temperate tract supported Blue Gum and his relatives—
lank, draped in fog, hell-bent roots
strangling public works.

Ranchers planted windbreaks, the phone company installed poles,
which respectively shattered in storms and sprang vital wires.
Even the railroad went crazy raising millions
of eucs for ties and tracks.
The ungrateful timber shrank, twisted, and cracked.
Shortly rotted.

Limbs dropped on gullible heads. Taproots shallow,
lateral roots buckled main roads. Trees keeled over on roofs.
Groves amassed oily tinder, flared into firestorms
at the flick of a butt.

Proclaimed a subversive curse, panicked victims
demand the once trusted species be outlawed,
never to shade this soil again. They yell:

Eucalyptus, you will kill us.

# The Wealth and Death in Mountains

*For months, the miners cannot see the sunlight*
*and many of them die inside the tunnels.*

–Pliny the Elder

The placer mining left ::
        tailings
        slag heaps
        dunes.

Where ::
        in meadows
        near oak and manzanita.

Pascal's barrel ::
        water-ruptured
        cavities drilled into rock.

*Ruina montium* ::
        wrecking of mountains,
        entrails of stone.

Tunneling and stoping ::
        veins of the
        mother lode.

Milk (not mother's) ::
        lead-laden ponds,
        toxic seep and leak.

Ponds (again) ::
      in them
      nothing growing.


Stream bed ::
      deposits
      ($$$).


[Overburden. Hushing.]


Hydrostatics ::


      why oil floats on water,
      why the surface is always flat
      whatever the shape of its container.


Pressure ::
      blood.

# Hail Mary

Sheet lightning illuminated the palm tree in the front yard
battling the sky with serpent heads and swords.
Wind scourged the oaks until they dropped leaves and branches
like they were giving up all possessions to a thief.

From within our power-less house, the rosary,
Hail Mary full of grace a chanted monotone
to hail stones beating the roof.
The Lord is with thee...

Clasped in a chain around our mother's legs
squeezing her veins, blessed art thou amongst women
and blessed is the fruit of thy womb.
(For our family, five times, the nurses exclaimed, "It's a girl.")

We don't know all the words to prayers that are not
Hail Mary's so the mantra breaks up
and then resumes.

We kept cutting off the blood
in our mom's calves, the rosary over and over.
Hail Mary, Mother of God, pray
for us sinners now, certainly now, and at the hour
of our death, maybe the death of our parents
and we'd be orphans locked up in foster homes.
Save us, Hail Mary!

We sang, a flat waterfall of voices.

I thought I saw Archangel Gabriel soar above the pasture,
wings flashing. "Hello! Here!"
He waves with a wobbly arm

and crashes into the neighbor's chimney,
teetering and blurring into the slant night.

Grace is a funny color that streaks through the curtains,
white like Mary's veil.

We envisioned next morning
trees uprooted, fences exploded, limp squirrels
clutching their last acorn.
We feared our father drowned in a tidal wave,
smashed near the bait and tackle shops
where he'd been selling fishing rods and lures.

Water shrinks with the ebbing tide
when the sun comes out as usual.
Father returns in his pickup truck.
Immigrant workers clear fallen trees.
Chainsaws and chippers fill the air
with their shattering roar.
The squirrels wake up and run away.

# The Sparrow Flies Away

Muscled branches of live oak overhang.
Plenty of birds perched, distracted
by the glint of handlebars.

Ready for the BB gun, forbidden-to-have.
My sisters back home eat Cheerios,
watch Scooby-Doo while parents sleep in.

I'm brave and perfectly balanced.
Rex, cow dog that came with our rented house,
sticks with me and my blue Schwinn.

Coursing beyond the red hardpan bank,
the off-limit canal where a boy drowned last winter.
I can't see the water from this gravel lane

that dead ends at the river
where every spring, aluminum boats
with fishermen overturn in the current.

Tiny dead bird would be a cruel trophy
to prove #1 girl can do anything she pleases,
not just squirt guns in the backyard.

Each shot misses on purpose
any warm-blooded thing.
Rex's perplexed eye fixes on me.

# Thought Safe

Keep bookmarks handy with maps of the world,
pieces of continents printed on them, places

you've studied and think you know
but are never sure of.

It's not what's printed on the bookmark that matters,
it's your ideas about the words the bookmark is keeping,

as if it were the world's thinnest safe
holding your thoughts

dry like powder, sprinkled into the card stock,
locked tightly until you return to where you were

before you went to work or turned off the stove.
Before you got busy with another interruption.

It's nice to be able to go back, where you left
patiently waiting for you to continue

your journey through the pages
even if you are not reading

old fashioned print on paper. What would it mean
to really lose your place?

# V.

# That Place That Isn't There Anymore

## Naive Tips About Lightning for the People of Aleppo

*The reason lightning doesn't strike twice in the same place is the same place isn't there the second time.*

—Willie Tyler

When you hear thunder,
you're within striking distance.
Find shelter.

Avoid tall structures.
Stay away from metal.

If you're in a boat,
get back to that place
that isn't there anymore.

# Horses in Dust and Ash

Here is a mare, duff-colored and mane-bedraggled, galloping ahead of a wall of airborne dirt. Texas Panhandle, 1938: She's driven to run a furious line, her nostrils smothering. The mare haunts me, like those workhorses in a hay field, rearing in front of volcanic tephra. South Iceland, 2010: I remember the caption: "The ash saved a lot of money on fertilizer and grass grows best where the most fell." Today I let the apple tree drop its full load of fruit. Rotting with wormholes where I haven't scooped them up, apples feed the soil within the root shadow. Maybe I will take better care, prune and cull for next season. Where my relatives live in Oklahoma is green and lush now, the old-timers buried with firsthand memories of the choked land. I've lost touch with that branch, visiting once at a hundred-year reunion. With my father I saw the old home church at the Oklahoma Land Run starting line. Our cousins decided not to save the family's sentimental congregation place, as if they even could. Let our landmark sink, return its disintegrating timber to the soil and weeds of forebears.

# The Battle for Another Middle Eastern Town

Frantic graves rise unheeded,
cross all borders nude,

shadows crowd the road
for a slice of bread

under cloud cover
vacant as bravery,

a needle threads
many ghosts waxen

through alleys
leaky, spilling

over the fright and burdens
unfolding courage

every time a car pulls over
this chant grief-ragged,

in the eyes of headlights
every pothole a wound.

# National Geographic Special

I had hoped to see an uncorrupted ice floe
shimmering below the aurora borealis,
polar bears sneaking up on seals, unfenced
caribou grubbing for lichen.

Instead I see Labradoreans sniffing gasoline,
their shacks in pools of it leaking
everywhere through dirty ice pack.
Below zero, Innu kids, pints of gas
sloshing in garbage bags pinched to their noses,
stagger, giggle, forget
the frozen expanse that traps them,
their indifferent government a laugh
away in the lit-up sky.

I see the Big Dipper in clear night
signal early spring, glow over this coastal island
Innu visited for centuries at winter solstice,
a respite from hunting deep within
the Labrador interior. They once celebrated
with *mukushan*, crushed
boiled caribou bones served in a bucket.
Ancestors visited, only visited, this
unsustainable place, to which nobody foretold
they'd be banished.

*Innu*, their word for human being, legends
splintering from lack of retelling. These Innu
marooned for decades on Davis Inlet, pack up
worn duffels for the new dwellings promised

on another shapeless tract of ice
to which they'll shift inland
and melt into the future.
Tracks left to vanish in slush.

# Millville

The tanned leather smell of wet oak
after my sleepover at your ranch.
You showed me sudangrass
you said contained cyanide, green blades
sharp as the shards of flint we hoped
were arrowheads. Sown at the edge
of pasture, the boundary thick and tall,
calves lost in it, their hide nicked until
they learned their way.

Your family's pool like inverted sky,
a mirage set against the parched foothills
strewn with truck-size boulders,
monuments to Mount Lassen.
The volcano on the horizon
we convince ourselves
will never again erupt.

## Ogallala The Great Aquifer Speaks to My Grandkids

They said the wells were innocent.
Drained of their essence by greedy furrows.

Every family protected a lush
lawn. Intervention was the last resort.

When the prairie's water was endless
the longitude and latitude of borders was a joke.

Stretching beyond the horizon you can never get to,
snow pack and floods were my food.

I refused to punish the wells and cisterns.
I never blamed the weather.

Rivers change course and my emptiness yawns
as your dust accumulates.

My three billion acres named after
a shrinking town, named after a scattered nation.

I'll be the desert. You be the plains.
Let's play hide and seek with all that nothing.

Ogallala runs off your tongue.

# R Was for Rhinoceros

An amusement park safari, futile anamnesis
of Africa's veld. Powdered keratin mixed into black tea
in vain, for virility, to cure hangovers…

The great banquet of body. Felled, his legs buckled, head
an open sore where horn was, dead eyes still
shining onyx, lashes like paint brushes dipped in vermilion.

Left to proliferate vermin, not his own species. R is for relic.
And when he's gone, a cavernous erasure as if this creature
never existed except in bestiaries and encyclopedias.

# Blowin' Cane

*For Othar Turner's "Shimmy She Wobble"*

Away in the Mississippi Delta,
far from my murky Sacramento
that drains into San Francisco Bay,
the last person blowin' cane
teaches his plump granddaughter.
She's but a kindergartner.

Old men pull beer from iced bottles,
goat turning on a spit,
pig smoked next to it, they tell
of the fife and drum

smuggled during the Civil War,
how they were chased
into hiding and then breath
pouring forth through holes
in hollowed-out rivercane
twining with
beat of the drum.

They hold that Africa begat
America, our babies bawl
Africa deep within
from people snatched
to seed this country, harvest
crops of our forebears.
They planted here,
they waded in silt
to baptize one another.

Shrill in our ears,
the strain weaves through air.
Drummers enter trances,
cousins shudder and chant.

Cane flute shoos away the past.

# Oakland

My grandfather drove a truck for the People's Bakery of Oakland,
went on strike for worker's rights in Oakland.

My mother played marbles, rode horses, sculled on Lake Merritt
when she was a girl in Oakland.

My father got stationed at Coast Guard Island, fell in love
with my mother at a dance in Oakland.

The earthquake wiped out my grandmother's girlhood street
when the freeway collapsed in Oakland.

There's no *there* there—I was slow to realize
Gertrude Stein was talking about Oakland.

# The Fabrication of Dobros

I dreamed Gibson moved its Dobro factory to China, worried what would happen to bluegrass music. Those Slav Dopyeras invented the Dobro in Los Angeles; *vaqueiros* packed them to Kona, rich sound made loud and affordable. The echoey twang and scratch of steel lazed in my dream, the sonance a riddle. I was caught up in America disintegrating, factories vacant, shops abandoned. Only malls full of gewgaws to buy. Tools, jeans, toys, every stick made in faraway continents. Dobro fret necks and bodies made there and every last thing made where I don't know anymore. This instrument I love to hear someone play. In a welter of acrylic and polyester dyed brightly I woke up sweaty, certain the ports of Oakland and L.A. had collapsed under laden containers stacked high like terrifying towers.

# Lion

Not even the riches of their teeth left
in the grass. Nor heads once big with manes.

Monsoon
torrents washing all away

until the children you could not save
become a cyclone

and the species of the savanna
exit the rays of our nervous system.

The natural world a martyr
to worship and torture again.

Trophies and talismans risen
to that other plane extolled in scripture and hymn.

# The Emperor and the Moth

Leaving me naked,

faint X across its folded body,
the moth lays eggs and multiplies
moth progeny to feast on my clothes,

lavish cloaks in my wardrobe.
The moth flies to its destiny
in darkness, as if jerked on a pulley.

Off with its head?
In a flutter of wings
mercy flees like a knave, gone

like insects crushed beneath my feet.
My infallible edicts have befallen millions,
I've had my fill of the day's offerings.

As the moth rests under my dimmed lamp
eyes like map pins appear to implore.
I want to pluck the threads of its feelers.

I want to pluck the threads of its feelers.
Eyes like map pins appear to implore
as the moth rests under my dimmed lamp.

I've had my fill of the day's offerings,
my infallible edicts have befallen millions
like insects crushed beneath my feet.

Mercy flees like a knave, gone
in a flutter of wings.
Off with its head?

In darkness, as if jerked on a pulley
the moth flies to its destiny,
lavish cloaks in my wardrobe.

The moth lays eggs and multiplies
moth progeny to feast on my clothes,
faint X across its folded body.

Leaving me naked.

# Notes

"Riven": Inspired by the history of eugenics in America, particularly in California and Oregon. Francis Crick, winner of the Nobel Prize for discovering DNA, in his letter from April 22, 1970 to Dr. Bernard D. Davis of Harvard Medical School:

> *My other suggestion is in an attempt to solve the problem*
> *of irresponsible people and especially those who are poorly*
> *endowed genetically having large numbers of unnecessary*
> *children. Because of their irresponsibility, it seems to me*
> *that for them, sterilization is the only answer and I would*
> *do this by bribery.*

"Chance of a Lifetime": "Pac Bell Park," refers to the first name that fans dubbed the baseball stadium in San Francisco, California. Since 2000, the stadium has served as the home of the San Francisco Giants. The park underwent a series of name changes during the time that SBC Communications purchased The Pacific Telephone & Telegraph Company and AT&T and negotiated naming rights. The current name is AT&T Park.

"My Grandmother's Bosom": In the Roaring 20s, fashionable young women known as flappers wrapped Ace bandages over their breasts to flatten their chests.

"Millville": The town of Millville in Northern California is located on Highway 44 near Lassen Peak, the southernmost active volcano in the Cascade Range and among the ten most dangerous in the United States. The last major eruption was on May 22, 1915.

"Oakland" ghazal: The Cypress Street Viaduct, often referred to as the Cypress Structure, was a 1.6 mile-long, raised two-tier, multi-lane freeway that was originally part of the Nimitz Freeway in Oakland, California. On October 17, 1989, a large portion of the structure collapsed during the Loma Prieta earthquake.

## About the Author

**Cathryn Shea** is the author of the chapbooks "Backpack Full of Leaves" (*Cyberwit*, 2019), "Secrets Hidden in a Pear Tree" (*dancing girl press*, 2019), and "It's Raining Lullabies" (*dancing girl press*, 2017). "Genealogy Lesson for the Laity" is her first full-length poetry book. Cathryn's poetry has been nominated for Sundress Publication's Best of the Net and appears in *New Orleans Review*, *Typehouse*, *Tar River Poetry*, *Gargoyle*, *Permafrost*, *Rust + Moth*, *Tinderbox*, and elsewhere. Cathryn is a fourth-generation northern Californian and lives with her husband in Fairfax, CA. She served as editor for *Marin Poetry Center Anthology*. For more information, see www.cathrynshea.com and @cathy_shea on Twitter.

## About the Press

Unsolicited Press is based in Portland, Oregon and is fueled by the dedication of hard-working volunteers. The press produces fiction, nonfiction, and poetry from emerging and award-winning authors.

Learn more at unsolicitedpress.com

CPSIA information can be obtained
at www.ICGtesting.com
Printed in the USA
LVHW100855071020
668175LV00004B/219